COOL
Makeup

How to Stage
Your Very Own Show

Karen Latchana Kenney

Consulting Editor, Diane Craig, M.A./Reading Specialist

ABDO
Publishing Company

Note to Adult Helpers

Makeup can really add to a costume, but it can get a little messy! To complete the activities in this book, kids are going to need some help.

Before beginning, find a good place for makeup application. Also, make sure kids test the makeup on a small portion of skin before applying it to their faces. This is very important for children with sensitive skin or allergies.

Hygiene is very important, so make sure kids do not share makeup or applicators. Make sure you have plenty of clean applicators and some towels to protect costumes and clothes. Help when needed, especially when kids are using makeup around their eyes. Set out some cleaning spray and paper towels for cleanup. Then stand by and see what kids can create with makeup!

Kids will need help removing the makeup as well. They will need washcloths, a gentle cleanser, and warm water.

Visit us at www.abdopublishing.com

Published by ABDO Publishing Company, 8000 West 78th Street, Edina, Minnesota 55439. Copyright © 2010 by Abdo Consulting Group, Inc. International copyrights reserved in all countries. No part of this book may be reproduced in any form without written permission from the publisher. The Checkerboard Library™ is a trademark and logo of ABDO Publishing Company.

Printed in the United States.
Design and Production: Colleen Dolphin, Mighty Media, Inc.
Photo Credits: Colleen Dolphin, Shutterstock
Series Editor: Katherine Hengel, Pam Price
Activity Production: Britney Haeg

Library of Congress Cataloging-in-Publication Data

Kenney, Karen Latchana.
  Cool makeup : how to stage your very own show / Karen Latchana Kenney.
    p. cm. -- (Cool performances)
  Includes webliography and index.
  ISBN 978-1-60453-715-4
  1. Theatrical makeup--Juvenile literature. I. Title.

PN2068.K44 2010
792.02'7--dc22

                                2009001752

Get the Picture!

There are many activities and how-to photos in this title. Each how-to photo has a color border around it, so match the border color to the appropriate activity step!

 activity step →

Contents

CREATING COOL PERFORMANCES

What's it all about?

Imagine putting on your very own show! Performing in front of an **audience** sounds fun, right? It is! You can pretend to be anything you want to be. Create an **illusion** through your costume, makeup, and stage. Tell a story by acting out a script. Put everything together, and you have a cool show!

You can create many kinds of shows. You can tell a funny story or a serious story. Put on a musical or a fairy tale. Creep out your audience with a monster or a ghost story. You can even be an alien on a strange planet!

Cool Performances Series

Cool Costumes

Cool Makeup

Cool Productions

Cool Scripts & Acting

Cool Sets & Props

Cool Special Effects

Permission

Make sure you have permission to put on a show. Ask an adult to help you set a makeup budget. Many drug stores and costume shops may sell discounted makeup.

Safety

Be careful when applying makeup to your eyes. Keep your eyes still and do not let makeup touch your eye. If you do get makeup in your eye, wash it with cool, clean water. If it is still **irritated**, tell an adult. Remember that you should not share makeup or applicators with other people.

Clean Up

After you apply your makeup, clean up your work space. Put covers on the makeup and put everything in a makeup case. Wipe down the surface you worked on with a wet towel. When you remove the makeup, use a washcloth, a gentle cleanser, and warm water.

Show Styles

There are many show styles. Shows can be one style or a combination of styles. Here are just a few.

Drama

Emotions are important in a drama. A dramatic show might be sad or it could make **audience**s laugh!

Fairy Tale

Fairy tales teach lessons. They have make-believe characters such as fairies, unicorns, and goblins.

Fantasy

Imaginary creatures make this kind of show fantastic! Mad scientists create monsters in laboratories, and aliens fly through space!

Musical

Singing is just as important as acting in a musical. Songs tell parts of the story.

THE MAGIC OF MAKEUP

One of the coolest parts of a show!

You've memorized your lines. Your costume is ready. Yet something is missing. Makeup! Makeup finishes your transformation.

Makeup can add years to your age. You can become an old man or woman! Or you might try becoming something not quite human! Playing with makeup can easily change how you look. It is definitely a cool and fun part of putting on a show!

Actors have used makeup for centuries. At first, they used materials such as chalk or **soot** on their faces. When stages were lit by candlelight, this rough makeup looked fine. Later, electric lights and gaslights lit the stage brightly. Because of the bright lighting, actors needed new makeup that made them look more **realistic** on stage. Today, specific makeup is made just for the theater.

Makeup designers apply makeup to actors. They study ways to make different looks. They can create a woman from the 1960s or a lion's face for a **Broadway** musical. Their tools are their makeup brushes and applicators. Theatrical makeup has vibrant colors and won't melt under the bright lights and heat on stage.

For your show, become your own makeup designer! Try some of the looks in this book. Check out the "Look the Part!" sections for variations to try. Experiment! Create completely new looks. There is no end to the cool characters you can create with makeup!

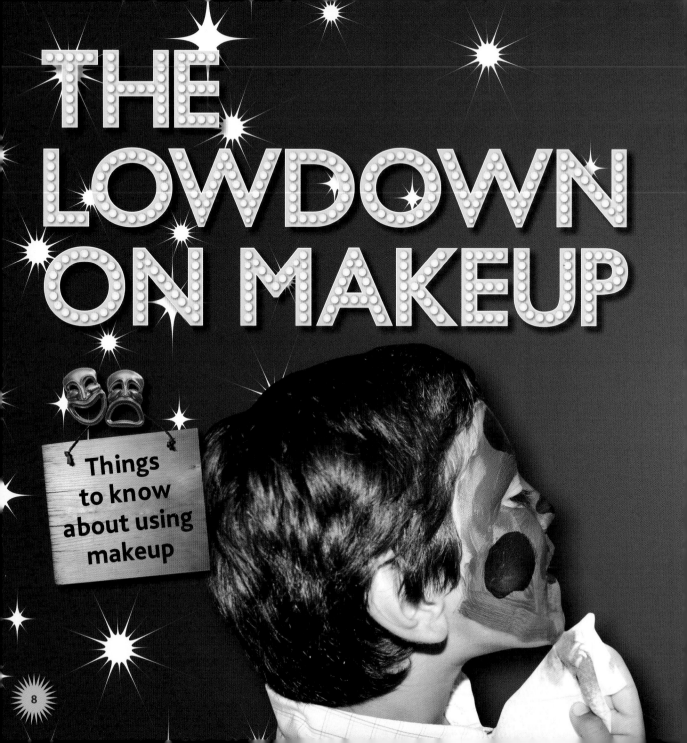

THE LOWDOWN ON MAKEUP

Things
to know
about using
makeup

Protect Your Face Put a small dot of makeup by your hairline. Wait for ten minutes. If your skin becomes red or itchy, you should not continue using that makeup.

Do not let makeup get into your eyes, nose, or mouth. Never share makeup with another person. Unclean makeup can **irritate** your skin. Most of the time, you will use makeup sponges and cotton swabs to apply the makeup. Always dispose of them when you are finished.

Squeaky Clean Start and finish with a clean, dry face. Wash your face with a gentle cleanser. Apply face moisturizer. Remember, leaving makeup on your face for long periods can irritate your skin. To keep skin healthy, always wash and moisturize your face before and after you apply stage makeup!

Apply It Find a space with a mirror and good lighting. You will also need a counter or table to put your supplies on. A bathroom is a good location for applying makeup. Always apply makeup after you have your costume on. Otherwise, you might smear your makeup while putting on your costume. Drape an old towel over your shoulders to protect your costume.

STAGE KIT

To complete the activities in this book, you will need these basic materials.

blush

eye shadow

cotton swabs

dark lip liner

eyeliner (black and brown)

face glitter

red lipstick

makeup brushes

face paint

makeup sponge

clean, unused sponge

scissors

Instant Old Age

Dark shading on a person's face creates the **illusion** of deep wrinkles and droopy skin. See how many years you can add with this look!

STAGE KIT

- brown eyeliner
- cotton swabs
- gray and white eye shadow
- dark lip liner

Start by wrinkling up your face. Use brown eyeliner to draw lines over the wrinkles. Now puff out your cheeks. Trace the line at the bottom of your cheek with eyeliner. Use a cotton swab to blend the lines into your skin.

 Apply gray eye shadow below your eyes and on your eyelids. Put white eye shadow over your eyebrows. Blend all the lines.

 Use a dark lip liner to make vertical lines on your lips. You look old!

Look the Part!

Put flour or baby powder in your hair to make it look gray! To make your hands look older, draw wrinkles on them! To be a witch, first cover your face with green paint. Then add the wrinkles.

Glamour Girl

STAGE KIT
- eye shadow in light and dark colors
- cotton swabs
- eyeliner
- makeup brush
- blush
- lipstick

Many productions call for a **glamorous** beauty of some sort. Here's how to **glam** it up!

Look the Part!

If you are playing a fairy, dust some face glitter on your cheeks! Experiment with different colors of eye shadow. See how they change your glamorous look!

14

1 Start with your eyes. Apply dark eye shadow along the crease of your eyelid. Then add lighter eye shadow above and below the crease. Blend the colors with a cotton swab.

Watch It!

Be careful! Your eyes are very sensitive. Pay close attention when putting on eye makeup. Ask an adult to help with eyeliner.

2 Darken your eyebrows with some eyeliner. Blend well. Ask an adult to apply eyeliner just above your eyelashes. The eyeliner should extend past the edge of your eye. It should curl up towards your eyebrow.

3 Use a makeup brush to apply blush on your cheeks. Finish by applying some lipstick. Beautiful!

Believable Beard

Disguise yourself with fake facial hair! Many professional actors add facial hair by using crepe hair. Crepe hair is a kind of fake hair made from wool. But you can also use makeup to create facial hair.

1 Cut out a square piece of kitchen sponge. Dampen the sponge with water.

2 Pat the sponge on the black face paint. Dab the bottom half of your face with the sponge. Keep going until it looks like you have beard stubble.

Mister Mustache

Try different mustache styles for different looks!

STAGE KIT
- black and brown eyeliner pencils
- cotton swabs

1 Use an eyeliner pencil to draw lines that mimic mustache hairs. Start in the middle, right under your nose. Move to one side of your mouth and then the other.

2 To create the **illusion** of many hairs, alternate between black and brown eyeliner. Carefully blend the lines with a cotton swab.

Wound & Bruise

To make **realistic** wounds, professional makeup artists use a special type of **silicone**. They mold the silicone to look like part of a person's face or skin. Using these easy makeup **techniques**, you can create similar looks!

STAGE KIT

- white, red, purple, blue, and yellow face paints
- black eyeliner
- makeup sponge
- small makeup brush

Using a small makeup brush, draw a thin line across your cheek or forehead with white face paint. Next to the white line, draw a thin red line.

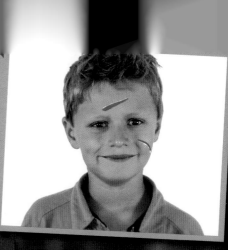

2

Use black eyeliner to make small, black x's over the lines. These are the stitches on your wound!

3

To make a bruise, start with a splotch of purple face paint. Blend the edges of the splotch into your skin with a clean makeup sponge.

4

Add some blue face paint to one side of the purple splotch. Then put some yellow face paint on the other side. Lightly blend the face paints with the makeup sponge.

Coolest Cat

Animals can take the leading roles in a production. In fact, cats are the only characters in the musical *Cats*.

STAGE KIT
- white and black face paint
- makeup sponge
- fine-tipped makeup brush
- black eyeliner
- red lipstick

Use a makeup sponge to cover your face with white face paint. Let the paint dry for a couple of minutes.

Choose a fine-tipped makeup brush and black paint. Draw a circle on the tip of your nose. Next, draw a line from the bottom of your nose to your upper lip. Apply red lipstick to your lips. Carefully outline your lips with black eyeliner.

Make three black dots on each side of the line under your nose. Then draw a line going out from each dot to create whiskers.

Look the Part!

Become a tabby cat! Use a makeup sponge to cover your face with orange or gray face paint. Then draw dark stripes on your face. The stripes should start near your nose and move out towards the edges of your face.

Using black eyeliner, draw a few whiskers coming out from your eyebrows. Then draw a line from the corner of your eye out towards your ear. Do this on both sides of your face. Meow!

21

Mousey Mug

Mice play major roles in the ballet *The Nutcracker*. A ballet uses dance, music, and scenery to tell a story.

STAGE KIT

- white, black, and gray or brown face paints
- makeup sponge
- fine-tipped makeup brush
- red lipstick

1 Use a makeup sponge to cover your face with gray face paint. Let the paint dry for a couple of minutes.

2 Using black face paint, draw a triangle on your nose. Then draw a line from the bottom of your nose to your upper lip. Fill in your upper lip with black paint.

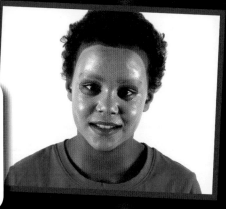

3 For the teeth, use white face paint to make a square. The square should cover your bottom lip. Let the white paint dry, and then outline your square with black face paint. Draw a vertical line in the middle so it looks like you have two teeth.

4 Draw two arches for eyebrows on your forehead. Add a dot of lipstick to each of your cheeks. Blend in the lipstick with a makeup sponge to create rosy cheeks.

5 Make three black dots on each side of the line under your nose. Then draw some whiskers. Squeak!

Angry Robot

This activity shows you how to turn a human actor into a robot. But some theaters don't use human beings as actors. They use actual robots instead!

STAGE KIT
- gray, white, and black face paints
- makeup sponge
- fine-tipped makeup brush

1 Use a makeup sponge to cover your face with gray face paint. Let the paint dry for a couple of minutes.

2 Draw a large rectangle around your mouth with white face paint. Paint everything inside the rectangle white, including your lips. Outline the white rectangle with black face paint. Let the paint dry for a couple of minutes. Then draw vertical lines across the rectangle.

3 Paint a white oval around each eye. Let the white face paint dry for a couple of minutes. Use black face paint to outline the ovals. Then paint two black rectangles above each eyebrow.

Wacky Alien

Aliens are out of this world! Aliens are often villains in productions, but they don't have to be! This activity shows how to make a funny alien, not a ruthless one!

STAGE KIT

- green, orange, and red face paints
- makeup sponges
- face glitter
- fine-tipped makeup brush

Use a makeup sponge to cover your face with green face paint. Let the paint dry for a couple of minutes.

Use a fine-tipped makeup brush to paint your lips orange. Add a red circle on your nose.

Make three small red circles on your forehead. Draw red lines on your cheeks. Add some face glitter to your circles and lines. Wacky!

Look the Part!

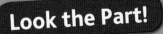

Spooky Skeleton

Ghost stories and other scary plays often have skeleton characters. Four skeletons dance and play music together in a graveyard in *The Skeleton Dance*. This Walt Disney cartoon came out in 1929.

STAGE KIT

- makeup sponges
- white and black face paints
- black eyeliner

Use a makeup sponge to paint your face white. Let the white paint dry for a couple of minutes.

 Now use a clean makeup sponge and black face paint to outline your face.

 Use black eyeliner to draw vertical lines above and below your lips.

 Carefully paint black circles around your eyes. You can overlap the white face paint.

 Finally, make your nostrils black. Spooky!

Look the Part!

Want to make a spooky shirt for your skeleton? Learn how in the *Cool Costumes* book.

CONCLUSION

Makeup can really transform you! Add a costume and acting **techniques**, and you can become a different character. It's easy and fun to experiment with makeup. Just use your imagination and let your face be the canvas!

But you need more than great makeup to put on a show. Check out the other books in the Cool Performances series to learn more about putting on a show. Practice your acting skills and try writing a script. Add a costume to complete your character's look. Create a super set and add special effects. Take it all on stage and put on a cool show. Remember, the coolest shows are the ones that are the most fun!

GLOSSARY

audience – a group of people watching a performance.

Broadway – a street in New York City that is home to many theaters.

glam – a very showy or extreme form of glamour.

glamorous – beautiful and exciting.

illusion – something that looks real but is not.

irritate – to make sore or inflamed.

realistic – seeming like the real thing.

silicone – a material used to make rubber and plastic.

soot – a black powder that is made when coal, wood, or oil is burned.

technique – a method or style in which something is done.

Web Sites

To learn more about putting on a show, visit ABDO Publishing Company on the World Wide Web at www.abdopublishing.com. Web sites about theater are featured on our Book Links page. These links are routinely monitored and updated to provide the most current information available.